I0503203

Copyright

Author: Robert Daudish

Publisher: Transcendence Publishing

This document is geared towards providing exact and reliable information in regards to the topic and issue covered. The publication is sold with the idea that the publisher is not required to render accounting, officially permitted, or otherwise, qualified services. If advice is necessary, legal or professional, a practiced individual in the profession should be ordered.

Dedication

To my loved ones and my wonderful readers…..

Table of Contents

Introduction

Throughout this book, it will pair each of the traditional steps in product development with a corresponding Acceleration tool that will make each step more cost efficient, less time consuming and most importantly more effective. Nowadays, technology allows us to be accessed worldwide, to work anywhere in the World. Your marketing and promotions can reach millions of people. Before, businesses were limited to their geography, the availability of experts were also very low limited.

Best practices in the e-business include value proposition, offshoring, contracting, website optimizing and more are discussed in this Kindle Book. Each of these services has unique comparative

tables and are provided to give you a better understanding in deciding which option to use.

This book begins with a discussion of the product development cycle. It will introduce to you new trends and concepts in the main phases of the development cycle. Along with these trends are the various online platforms that will help you to augment these trends through automation and delegation. These platforms are easy to use and are pretty cheap.

Whether you want your startup business or not, this book will provide you with a working knowledge on how to do it. Even with the potential of automating and delegating your business processes, you will also see the value of being a hands-on proprietor. You should always expand your knowledge and skills.

This book can only go so far as to provide you with the basics and some advanced principles and techniques in product development and the available power tools at your disposal. As soon as you apply the principles in this guide, experience will take over as your teacher and business mentor. However, when you seem to forget those

websites that can help you with outsourcing your advertising projects or you could not remember what SEO of the company stands for, this Kindle Book will always be here to remind you the basics.

Chapter One: Consider and Believe

In this chapter you will acquire information about:

- How to be The 21st Century Entrepreneur
- How to Materialize Your idea
- Lifecycle of Your Product

The importance of entrepreneurship is now made more apparent by different factors, from popular culture, the economy and seek for profit. Popular TV shows, Shark Tank, Dragon's Den and The Profit are shows that give opportunities to participants to announce their business idea to a panel of potential investors. These shows are meant to portray the interaction between entrepreneurs and tycoons along with the contestants' process of creating and selling their business idea.

The recent economic crises also present the necessity of having more than one source of income. When big employers started declaring bankruptcy and fired several employees, the need for a personal source of income through business became more important than ever. Nowadays, it is not a matter of having one or two jobs, but

instead having an own business that can generate money is being used as a contributing factor towards financial freedom and security.

In my opinion, entrepreneurship satisfies the desire for profit. Entrepreneurs desire for new experiences and adventures. The thrill of doing something new that is outside of their comfort zone is only enhanced by the bonus of profit and the chance to earn money.

The objective of this chapter is to give you a foundation on the basics of product development. It presents the traditional steps and techniques an entrepreneur must take to turn his idea into reality. If you are a beginner in entrepreneurship, you may want to read thoroughly on the contents of this chapter. If you already have an experience as an entrepreneur, you can browse through the contents and move forward on the next chapter.

How to be The 21st Century Entrepreneur

The stereotype of an entrepreneur has been repeatedly challenged for the past decades. Due to globalization, the stereotype has been replaced with a new profile of the modern entrepreneur. Before, if someone talked about entrepreneurship, you imagined a picture of a person with an MBA, wearing a suit and a tie, while going to his business in the middle of town. He advertises his business in newspapers or flyers; he pays for overhead expenses such as staff salaries and office utilities and makes good money for his family.

Today entrepreneurs come from all ages and backgrounds. You don't need anything much to start your own business. You can manage your business at the comforts of your home while wearing casual shirts and jeans. You do not have to spend a single cent to advertise your business. You can be in your office 24/7 without physically being there at all. The power of internet!

The modern entrepreneurs are very smart; they have accounts on most social media and on most online retailers. They are open to change and seek new gadgets and updates in the features. They are

multi-taskers, while they may have their regular day jobs, they can run their businesses at the same time. Even mothers, who raise their families, students, who are at school, and a group of friends with a common passion but without time to be together, can manage their businesses at the same time. They see challenges as **opportunities for growth** and change and improvement as necessary.

However, they must share one thing in common and that is **passion**. This is the drive that will motivate them to pursue their endeavor, while experiencing the ups of profits or the downs of losses. Passion is important, because this is the thing that will get them through the challenges of their business and give them courage in the face of its risks.

Every great dream begins with a dreamer. Always remember, you have within you the strength, the patience, and the passion to reach for the stars to change the world.

Harriet Tubman

How to Materialize Your Idea

Entrepreneurs may be unable to focus all the time. They have so many ideas for business that they spread their skills and resources too much. Entrepreneurs cannot filter their thoughts. Their obsessive compulsive behavior is the reason of that. They may also choose business ideas that are very much outside their line of expertise and comfort zone. They may also lack the motivation, initiative and passion to pursue the endeavor. They need a mentor or a coach.

Despite the millions of people, each with great business, product and service ideas, there are also millions of cases when they fail to turn their ideas into reality. There are many reasons why these situations occur, such as external factors, for example, the economy, the current industry or the saturation of the market. It can also be the presence of strong almost unbeatable competitions. These competitions are firmly entrenched in the daily lives of your target customers that you can no longer share the market. There can also be a vast amount of supply that the demand of the product or the service may not be enough to make profit out of it. These are factors that are

outside their control and these entrepreneurs cannot blame themselves for failing to realize their dreams.

On the other hand, when these people with their bright ideas cannot bridge the gap between idea and materialization is because of the lack of skills and guidance of the process. They have in their hands something unique or something that is on a totally different level compared to similar products or services. However, because of insufficient information, lack of knowledge or the absence of a proper guidance, they fail in realizing their dreams. There is one major difference between these set of internal reasons and the previous paragraph's external factors. These internal factors are within the entrepreneur's control and taking control of them may be the key to business success.

With all the ideas running in the entrepreneurs mind, it is easy to lose track of their inspirations or become distracted with other thoughts. Do not allow memory failure or distraction to steer you away from realizing your business idea. If you are in the habit of imagining and brainstorming during your idle time, here are the top 10 ways to make sure you never miss out on an "eureka" moment:

1. Write or sketch it in a notebook.

2. Share it with a trusted friend and talk it over

3. Have a voice recorder app if you prefer speaking out your idea.

4. Use sticky notes to post your ideas into a wall that can always remind you

5. Download a diary or notepad app in your mobile phone.

6. Use color codes to organize and differentiate one idea from another

7. Put all of your notes in one place instead of scattered around in your area

8. Use your voice answering machine to record your own ideas

Every entrepreneur must be able to predict the potential of their ideas but there is a difference between simple speculation and an intellectual guess. Simple speculation may involve too many idealistic and fantastic dreams. These fantasies are not grounded on any facts, statistics or business research. These ideas sound great and perfect, but their execution is almost either impossible or unprofitable for you.

Each person has a wealth of creative energies within themselves, all we have to do is to open them. What they have in creativity, they may lack in guidance. It is important to channel all these positive energies into a tool that can focus their thoughts, filter their ideas and soon realize their business dreams.

Lifecycle of Your Product

There is significant work and effort required to transform your idea into reality. However, it is worthwhile to go through the process since this is the make or break situation for your business. This is where you will be able to focus, filter and formulate your idea into a solid business plan.

There are generally 8 steps in product development and each stage has their own tools to complete it.

1. Generation Using SWOT Analysis

2. Screening Using Forecasts, Trends and Feasibilities

3. Development and Testing Using Prototyping and Contracting Professionals

4. Business Analysis Using Pricing and Profitability

5. Beta and Market Testing Using Mockups and Packaging

6. Manufacture Using Estimation, Logistics and Contingencies

7. Commercialization Using Advertisements and Promotions

8. Review and Refine Using Introductory Pricing, Competition and Forecasting

This is the first stage of the product development lifecycle. You subject your idea into rigorous test - SWOT. For example, you want to present a new line of fashion accessories. Your target market can be men, women, and adults, and adolescents. You can either find twenty adult women and group them in one batch or make sure that you have each target market represented in one group. Prepare a list of focus questions prior to the test. Ask questions to them and document their answers and reactions. Make sure you are able to trace which opinions or comments belong to which demographic.

Strengths, Weaknesses, Opportunities and Threats or SWOT are another tool that you can use when you generate your idea. Assess your own idea, what are its weaknesses? Opportunities for your product may be an untapped market or a gap in consumer options. Threats can be logistics or legislation that may interrupt your production or delivery.

SWOT worksheet looks like this:

SWOT ANALYSIS

	Helpful to achieving the objective	Harmful to achieving the objective
Internal origin (attributes of the organization)	Strengths	Weaknesses
External origin (attributes of the environment)	Opportunities	Threats

As you go through this process, you now have information that will either allow you to abandon, refine or pursue your idea. This is the reason why this first stage is important, you can make changes even before you start production and use money or other resources. The time you will spend in doing these activities will have significant effects down the road and it will prove that they are time well spent.

Now that you have input from your preliminary research using SWOT, it is now time to eliminate imperfections and refine the features of your product. Your tools for this step are forecasting and feasibilities. While SWOT will provide you with current information and opinions, the next task should attempt to assess the future of your product. Some questions that you can ask yourself for this step are:

1. How accessible or replicable is your product?

2. What is the status of the manufacturing industry, can it create your product?

3. Will there be future competition for your product?

4. What are the chances for growth in this product?

5. How will the market decrease or increase in the future?

Based on the inputs of your target market and the results of your research, do you require making changes in your idea? Are you willing to make change? **How far will you compromise your dream to satisfy the market, customers and yourself?**

These are very important questions that you have to answer as early as you can. There are things when you overhaul your idea just for the purpose of meeting the demands of the facts and figures, but in the end, you will feel that it is no longer your idea, you might even feel disappointed. The effect is that you lose your motivation or sense of ownership of the idea. The very drive that triggered your entrepreneurship may be gone because of how far you have compromised your vision for future.

Whether you are a beginner or an experienced entrepreneur, there are times when individuals report an instinct or a gut feeling that their idea is right despite the criticisms and findings. Sometimes your feeling is wrong and sometimes it is right. Make sure you are able to make an informed decision on your product development but do not

let it force you to decide on something that will make you unhappy. **Remember, there is a thin line between confidence and arrogance**, one can genuinely point you towards the right path and the other may prevent you from making the best possible outcome for you

> Opportunities are usually disguised as hard work, so most people don't recognize them.
>
> *Ann Lannders*

.

Idea of Your Product

Before you start with the prototype, there is an important factor that you have to take into consideration; you must devote your full attention and time into this since there is absolutely no room for error. It doesn't matter how perfect your idea seems, due to the results of your research, refinements and compromises, you have to validate its originality. This is where intellectual property and patents come into play. This is not only a matter of originality, but also a matter of protection.

Patents are filed in the government to represent your ownership of an idea. This is your legal tool that you can employ to prevent others from making, selling or copying your idea. The same way this patent protects you; it also protects others who may have already developed the same idea that you have. You cannot say that you have already thought of the idea since you were a child and the other person just thought of it a few years ago. The basis of awarding is the first person who files it in the government and proves his ownership of the idea.

Each government and country will have their own provisions in the awarding of patents. For example, in the US only a person may apply for a patent, but the patent itself can be owned by a person or a corporation. Although, you can assign the development of your idea to another person, and you can prepare legal documents such as employment contracts that bar your employee from claiming rights to your idea. Currently most countries, including the US has a patent office in charge of intellectual property. However, patents, by their nature as being awarded by a government, is only restricted to the actual country that issued it. This means your idea can only be protected in the country where you issued the claim. However, the World Trade Organization is in the process of interconnecting their patent laws and database to create a universal system that protects entrepreneurs and their ideas, regardless of their nationality.

How to Price Your Product or Service properly

Now that you have a working idea on the specifications and the cost of your product, you can begin analyzing the product in terms of monetary figures. This is where profit and profitability come into play.

There is an entire school of thought on pricing. The challenge is finding and choosing pricing principles that are appropriate to you, your product and your market. For example, one pricing principle states that the price of your product must be within the price range of similar products in the market. For example, if most leather bags are within the thirty to fifty dollar range, then your custom made bag must also be within the average. Anything more will discourage your buyers from choosing your product over the other.

On the other hand, there is another pricing principle that states the more expensive your product is, the more chances your customers will choose it. This is because consumers today associate price with value and quality. A low priced product is assumed to have substandard quality of materials, poor craftsmanship and generally a cheap product. The opposite is also true. If a product has a high price, it is thought to be made of high quality materials, accessible and chosen only be the elite few and generally a better product. This principle states that the more expensive you price the product, the more valuable and highly desired it will appear to the consumers.

You can also target markets to provide you with information on the price aside from comparing your price with other products. At times, customer feedback is as important as the market trends themselves. You can make your own research by searching the Internet for similar products and find the average costs. Incorporate these findings to triangulate and validate your price, your sources are your own research, your consumers and the prices of your own market.

If you are a beginner or you are introducing something untested in the market, it is way better to play it safe by using the average as the basis of your price range. On the contrary, if you have already established yourself in the market and made a name of your own or of your brand, then you can take more risks in the pricing of your product.

Whether you chose a average or higher than average pricing scheme, you must add all these figures to determine your profitability. These prices become your revenues and the cost to sell them becomes your expenses.

Determine your profit margin during this stage. Would you want to double your earnings or gradually build on your profit? If there is a significant amount of investment what is your timetable to break-even and claim profits? Another important consideration is the volume you need to sell or the revenue you need to receive based on your target margins. If you are able to simulate these cash flows and make them as accurate as possible, you can have a better perspective of not only the potential of your product but also additional information on how you can modify the prototype to suit your margins.

For example, say you have an apple pie as a product. The only way you can differentiate it from other products in the market is by using organic apples and all natural ingredients. However, the effect will be a higher cost for production. If you insist on the ingredients, you risk lower sales and thus lower profits. On the other hand, if you opt

for compromising other ingredients, you can keep production costs low, price your product lower to meet your profit margins. However, your product will lose its key difference from other products and may suffer down the road.

The importance of this step is to give you an appreciation of the financial side of product development. **Remember it is not only, brainstorming, drawing and testing, you must give yourself time to sit and do the math.** Some entrepreneurs have the knack for numbers and some do not. Having an accountant or a mentor can help you in this step. These professionals can provide you with budgets, income streams, expense items, legal fees and other payments that must be part of your budgeting.

About Packaging

Another extremely important process in this step is the product packaging. Aside from the actual functions of packaging such as protection of your product, compression and other physical risks to your product, it is the secondary function that is highly valuable. Packaging does not only provide information about your product, but also entices customers to consider purchasing your product. This is where you can strategize how to market and present you product in the most eye catching way possible and preferably stick out in a line of similar products in a shelf or in an online platform. This is where you can communicate to your potential customers your brand, identity and uniqueness of your products compared to other similar items in the market. Related to packaging is the point of sale display. Convenience and portion control are also considerations when you develop your product package. Aside from making your product look good through your packaging, it must also provide convenience when you distribute, ship, stack, store, reuse or dispose. If you have a consumable product, you have to make use of portion control. On what sizes will you make your product? How will they be

dispensed? How can the packaging conform to government standards? Every way to maximize a package must be made, for example, most shampoo bottles are shaped to control the amount dispensed per use. It is also shaped so that an average person can grasp it comfortably and without slipping in the shower.

About Manufacturing

This part requires expert inputs. If your product needs to be created from scratch, you will need to send technical specifications to the manufacturers along with a product safety data sheet. These data will be required by the factory that will make your product. This is not only a list of materials that are needed but actual quantities, sizes, weights and other measurements that will be part of the production line. Depending on your manufacturer, the specifications you provide must meet certain standards for them to even accept your product.

In this step, your team of professionals will be of great help to you, specifically an industrial engineer. This professional can help you turn your prototype or mockup into the real deal. His expertise is in the line of integrating the 4Ms for every manufacturing project. He can link together money, manpower, machinery and materials that will result to your product. He can prepare not only the technical documents that you need to submit to your manufacturer but also much more. Depending on his expertise and your need, he can prepare the process flow for your product, control resources and design and optimize your product depending on your requirements and specification. If you are not an engineer yourself or if you do not have the capacity to take on the more technical side of the manufacturing of your product, these industrial engineers will be of great help to you and you should not go without one.

The heart of this stage is the manufacturers. You will need a network of factories and point persons to turn your idea into the real thing. Aside from that you will need to gather quotations on the best deal that you can make. They will expect you to provide quantities, detailed descriptions, materials, colors, finishes, dimensions, weight, sizes and other possible specifications. Your creative team can provide these details for you. Your task is to find the factory that can manufacture the products. Use procurement standards to help you choose the best manufacturer for you.

Another tool that you have to make use of is logistics. You may have the best product with the best price and best packaging but if it cannot reach your potential customers or market in a timely and efficient manner, you may lose money, customers and even your business. Logistics involves a wide range of systems, from material

handling, inventory, transportation, storage and warehousing and also security. So broad is the concept of logistics that it already has its own specializations. Often called logisticians, these are experts who specialize in specific areas of the supply chain process, from procurement to distribution professional who are employed when dealing with suppliers and delivery of products. Disposal and reuse logistics are used to move surplus or waste made by your product. Green logistics are made to consider impact on the environment and emergency logistics are for critical events such as anticipated delays in the chain.

1.   Logistic capability and presence of contingency measures

2.   Presence of dedicated account managers

3.   References or reviews from other clients and track record

4.   Capacity to serve your need

5.   Quality, price and timeliness of their work

Aside from price per every item, you also need to take into consideration other charges that your manufacturer may hide from you. Shipping, handling, insurance, commissions and other expenses

will be charged to you and often are not included in the price per item. Another consideration is the time. **Can your manufacturer deliver not only quality items but also in a timely manner?** What are the provisions to protect you from failures on their end. Try to get three quotations from different manufacturers to give you better chances of making the right decision.

About The Launch and Promotions

Your campaign must satisfy the needs of a customer prior to a purchase. These are: awareness, knowledge, liking, preference, conviction and finally the actual purchase. In this model, a consumer moves from one step to another until he reaches the decision to purchase. This can be a superficial or passing memory of your product. Once the consumer has the awareness, he is now ready for more facts and figures, such as price, benefits, comparison to other products and other knowledge. **Your campaign must be able to make your product desirable than other competitors.** Once the customer has all of these, he can convince himself to make the decision, the customer will buy from you. From then, he will choose and purchase your product. With these customer needs in mind, prior to the purchase, you must make sure that your advertising campaign can satisfy these customer expectations.

When you have the product, designed, packaged, priced and delivered, it is now time to launch, advertise and promote it. Marketing your product is your communication tool to persuade and convince your potential customers to become buyers. This is where

you put together your brand, slogan, themes, packaging, collaterals, mass media and other promotions into a powerful marketing campaign.

Review Your Product and Refine it.

To promote your product, it is important to sell it at an introductory price first. Although, this may mean a small profit margin, you must view it as an investment. You need to get your product sold and into the houses or uses of your customer. This will produce a multiplier effect and a returning customer effect. If your product is truly the best in the market and wins over your competition then your customers will act as promoters of your own product. Word of mouth will happen and soon your product may even become a new trend. When you prove your product, your customers will return and patronize your business. These effects will not be possible if you started with a high price.

Another important effect for getting your products out is that you can use the sales as a baseline for your forecasting. How many were sold in a week? Which places had the most sales? These are all very important data that you can collect and use to anticipate your product's life for the future. When you see a steady increase in acceptance of your product, you must modify it and increase its value and also replace the introductory with a more competitive price.

Measure the sales and other product data in terms of volume, revenue and profit. From these you can have an intelligent guess on how your product will perform in the next quarter and even in the next year. From these predictions, you can make appropriate business decisions, such as product design improvement, re-pricing and even new product spin-offs. Once you have the need for a spin-off product or for an improved product, it will be a new product to design and the entire product development cycle starts again.

Chapter Two: Creation of Your Masterpiece

In this chapter you will acquire information about:

- More About Product Development

- About Market Research

- Outsourcing

- Making Your own Brand

The previous chapter was about building the right foundation for your product development. It was meant to introduce you to the basics of manifesting your idea into reality. Now that you have a solid base, you can build on it with advanced and modern tools for product development. In this chapter author will discuss advanced topics in product development, using new trends and best practices and will tell you about acceleration tools, that will help you in your product development and in your business.

More About Product Development

As a businessman, You must be able to differentiate yourself and your product from the rest of your competitors. While other entrepreneurs may follow the same product develop lifecycle, you can make a unique product through value proposition.

When all products are made towards customer satisfaction, your product must go beyond satisfaction. Your value proposition must target customer delight. This means that during your product development you must take into account not only giving the bare minimum that all other products in the market are also doing. Your product must also be capable of providing something special and unique that will convince your customers to choose you and your product above all others.

This is where value proposition comes into scene. A customer value proposition is the total value that you promise to exchange to your product with your customer's money. It is also your statement that says your product is different from your competitors. If your product shares similarities with others in the market, how can you refine to make it stand out?

Take for example the coffee served by Starbucks. Coffee is pretty much served in almost every dinner, but what made the franchise successful is how it was able to distinguish itself from competition. Starbucks unique value propositions were made of three components. High quality coffee, they did not just source coffee, but they actually partner with coffee growers and provided specifications on how to grow, roast and deliver their coffee beans. The second was customer intimacy. Baristas are trained to remember the names of their regulars along with their usual favorites. The final component is the atmosphere. Starbucks prides itself in their statement, people came to Starbucks for the coffee but they stayed for the atmosphere. These three components created a compelling value proposition that made Starbucks unique from all other coffee shops. In fact, other coffee shops use the Starbucks model to increase their chances of business success. Today, Starbucks is installing Duracell Powermat on its tables. This will allow customers to charge their phones as they drink their coffees. This is another unique customer value

proposition that Starbucks is implementing by developing a new service to its customers.

Now, review your output in your product development cycle. Include a customer value proposition in the equation. Make sure that what you add is something unique or never been heard of in your product and competitors. You may not be able to imitate the scale of Starbucks' value proposition but you can take inspiration from their creativity and focus on customer delight.

About Market Research

One of the most successful companies in the US is Apple. According to Steve Jobs, his company does not do market research. He is often quoted as saying that "You can't just ask customers what they want and then try to give that to them. By the time you get it built, they'll want something new." As an entrepreneur, the lesson that you can learn from Jobs is that you must able to use market research and prospecting to anticipate the needs and wants of your target customers. When you are able to forecast the demand, you are in the better or even the first position to supply it.

Another tool that entrepreneurs can use is market research. You must be able to distinguish market research with marketing research. Although it is used interchangeably, experts suggest differentiating between the two. Marketing research is interested on the marketing side of the business, such as the process and systems that you can set up to link yourself with your customers.

On the contrary, market research is all about maintaining your competitiveness through studying the needs, wants, size and

behavior of your market. This is where you also differentiate your customers into segments, based on gender, age, economic status, personality, purchasing behavior, interests and other demographic data. This is meant to modify your product into something that will suit the demand of your target demographic.

Prospecting is a term borrowed by entrepreneurs from the mining industry. While miners dig in different locations in the hopes of finding gold, entrepreneurs use prospecting to make strategic conversations to generate interest and create sales.

Outsourcing

Production offshoring, a specific term used when you relocate your manufacturing to another country, is currently very advantageous in China. There are many reasons why China holds the top rank in the offshoring industry. The obvious reason is the cost, labor, production and logistics are significantly cheaper in China than anywhere else. Another reason is that the offshoring industry is already set up. The country has decades of experience in the offshoring industry and reached its peak in 2005 when companies came in droves to China. Factories and professionals are already in China to serve your production needs.

In 2015, China expects to have a 25% increase in its offshoring services and entire cities are being built to satisfy the delivery and logistic support needed for the products. In fact 10 to 15 years from now, labor costs are expected to remain favorable to entrepreneurs. Compared to India, Brazil, Philippines, Vietnam and other popular countries for outsourcing, China offers diversification, low risks and attrition that could harm your product. If you plan to offshore some of your business processes to another country, China is one of the best options.

Traditional manufacturing or sourcing of your products and services were once limited to the locale or geographic boundaries where you belong. Manufacturing partners were often domestic in nature. As a result of globalization and the interconnection of economies of one country to another, offshoring has become a possible alternative. In offshoring, you can relocate a business process to another country. You can offshore major or a minor process, from manufacturing, packaging, customer service, clerical to even accounting processes. The primary reason behind offshoring is to reduce costs, which in turn increases your profit margin.

Nowadays, the leading countries which received off-shored contracts are China for manufacturing, telecommunications for India and software and graphics development for the rest of the Brazil, Russia along with India and China.

Making Your own Brand

Aside from prototyping and packaging, there is another important concept that you have to apply in your business. Branding takes into consideration not only the tangible elements of your product, such as price, package and the product itself but also the intangible elements. Some of the elements are experience, emotions and association. The goal of branding is to build customer awareness and loyalty to your product through your product's unique identity.

Each brand is different but has the same basic elements:

1.   Name

2.   Tagline

3.   Logo

4.   Figures, Shapes & Graphics

5.   Colors

6.   Sounds, scents, tastes and motion when applicable

When you choose the name, you may choose from many styles. You can use the initials of your company; use words that rhyme, or verbs

that evoke desired actions or feelings. You can use your own name or the place where the product originated. You can use fictional names too. For the tagline, use as few words as possible that can represent the product's features or benefits, you can also make it as a call to action to your customers or stimulate feelings and emotions. Logos and other graphics must have high memory retention and association value. It has reached a degree of awareness that it is often used interchangeably with photocopy. Remember, there is no stable formula for branding. What you must do is to make sure that your brand and your employees serve to communicate your product to your potential customers.

Elance®

oDesk

Use these acceleration tools that are made possible by the Internet and modern technology to help you with the difficult steps in product development. odesk and elance are two of the worlds most popular global work platforms that connect individuals from a wide variety of professions to entrepreneurs who require their expertise and experience. These platforms are your power tools that you can use to create a contractual creative team for your product development. You must not ignore these two power tools if you intend on saving hundreds if not thousands of dollars during your product development process.

These two platforms work similarly by allowing you to interview, review samples and portfolio along with the profile of each professional, called a freelancer. You post your requirement in a job description window. You can categorize it depending on your need, whether writing, product designing, software and web development, customer service, business services, administrative support and other professional requirements. You can set a price range and deadline for your offer as well as the specifics of the work you are offering. Here you will be able to find an industrial designer, graphic designer, packaging designers that will contribute in bringing your product to life.

Once you receive proposals from freelancers, you will see their profile, reviews from other clients, the price they will charge and the timeframe they can deliver. You can compare the experiences, prices and other facts about your applicants before making the choice. You can send messages to your applicants through odesk and elance without revealing your personal emails. Once you have accepted a proposal, your payment will be put in escrow. Take note that the release of funds is entirely within your control. Even if your freelancer already sent through completed work, this will not trigger the release of funds. These platforms will charge freelancers a commission for every payment made. While odesk will deduct it

from their freelancers, elance will charge the commission to your account.

For example, if you need an industrial engineer, these platforms will be your best alternative to find one. Check their profile, their work experience and other background. Another important part of their profiles that you need to look at are the reviews that they receive from their clients. These platforms make use of a 5 star rating system, the more stars the better the reviews. Look also at their portfolio; is their design aesthetic similar to what you have in mind for your product? If you want specific qualifications, you can filter your search to show only industrial engineers experienced in technical design, from a specific country say the US and a specific rate that you are willing to pay. Odesk and elance make it possible for contractors, who are living abroad, to still receive gainful employment. Although they may be geographically separate from you, you can still access their experience and expertise.

Take note aside from a fixed price, you can offer them an hourly rate. These platforms will provide you with tools to monitor their actual work hours so you will only pay them for the time they

worked on your project. However, it is still best to choose a fixed price contract. Make sure you agree on the cost to save you from headache down the road. This will prevent disputes on payment. To protect you, odesk has a feature called milestones that will allow you to send payment in batches based on the completed work. Since release of payment is entirely within your control, you can dispute work quality, timeliness and communication with the platforms' support team to protect you just in case you encounter problems with your freelancer.

Various Advertising Techniques

You have several options that you can choose from for your advertising needs, they can range from the usual to the creative, from the free to the inexpensive and from the traditional to the modern. Free does not necessarily mean no money spent but it can also mean you can do it yourself. Here are some of them:

Free:

1.   Word of mouth

2.   Posting on different forums

3.   Press releases

4.   Facebook/Twitter

5.   Blogs

6.   Samples

7.   Google place

8.   Yellow pages (Online)

9.   Ad swaps

10.   Volunteer for ad space

Nothing beats testimonials from satisfied customers to advertise your products. Never underestimate the power of customers to refer your product to their friends or colleagues. You can add incentive to this word of mouth option by giving a discount for every successful referral.

You can write short articles and distribute them to your local press. They are always looking for new products to feature in their lifestyle section.

If you visit a forum or a blog that is all about the product or service you are selling, you can post links to your site or the address of your store. Members of the forum or followers of the blog will be able to click on that link and see that address on their next visit. As powerful as word of mouth is, social media has definitely a wider reach. Post your product and tag and share as many times and as often as you can.

Samples are another way of free advertisement, go to strategic places to give away your samples. Some websites allow you to swap ads, you post an ad on their site but you have to post their ad on yours.

Another free way to get ad space is to volunteer for local organizations or causes. You can negotiate for a spot in their newsletter or on their next meeting.

Low Cost:

1.   Google ads

2.   Local directories and community sites

3.   Flyers and brochures

4.   Various discount coupons

For low cost paid ads, you can always rely on both print and web-based media. Google ads can charge you for as low as $10 a day to attract customers both locally and globally. The best thing about Google ads is you only pay for every click. The traditional advertising tools cost varies but can be more expensive than their online counterparts. Aside from that they also do not have the same reach as web-based advertisements. Discount coupons have a double effect both as an advertising tool and a sales tool.

Facebook with its billions of registered users is the most effective and suitable way to promote your product or service. The service that Facebook provides is free, easy for you to use and most importantly easy too for your network to share to their own network of friends. It allows you the maximum benefit of an online advertisement, text, pictures, videos, location, contact details, reviews and feedbacks. It has both computer and mobile applications making it accessible in and outside the home.

Facebook has finally opened its platform for advertising. It allows for finely tuned targeting based on the profiles of its users. This is where the benefit of utilizing paid advertising in Facebook can be found and this is what makes it different from traditional media. Not only will it allow you to specify which users will see the advertisement but also on the exact time frame or period. When you have these parameters, Facebook will automatically give you a quoted price for the cost.

There are several options that you can choose from for Facebook advertising. There are adverts, targeting, boosted posts and Facebook offers. Adverts place your ads directly in the News Feed or on the

right side panel of every Facebook user. The wider reach you want, the more expensive it will be. The best option is to start with a target audience. In targeting, you can send your Facebook ad depending on a set of parameters. It can be based on location, demographic, connection, purchasing behaviors and interests. For example, your product is an innovated kitchen utensil; you can target users who are mothers, with cooking interests and have bought similar items in Facebook. If you already have an online store, you can choose a boosted posts package. When you post your website link on your page, you can make it appear not only on your page or your friend's page but also on other news feeds too. Finally Facebook Offers create a virtual coupon that they can bring to your shop or use in your online store discount screen. The good thing about this feature is that the coupons can be shared by users to their friends.

There is no set amount for the price of a Facebook advertisement. Instead, the rates are governed by an ever changing system based on the advertising needs fellow entrepreneurs like you. For example, the more advertisers are targeting this specific demographic that you also want to target, the more expensive it will be. Facebook has two

models that you can from for your advertising needs, CPM or cost per thousand impression and CPC or cost per click. In CPM, you pay when 1,000 people have seen your advertisement. In CPC, you pay when someone clicks your advertisements. Although these are the factors to consider, on the average, each advertisement ranges from $.05 to $5 per click.

Facebook may have varying rates in advertisements but it will provide you with an estimated cost based on the parameters that you will set. Regardless of the cost, comparative studies show that Facebook is still the cheapest in advertising. While in newspapers, it will cost you $32 to reach 1000 people; in Facebook it will only cost you $.25

Chapter Three: Managing Everything

In this chapter you will acquire information about:

- Do The Most Important Tasks Yourself
- Networking

Do The Most Important Tasks Yourself

With all the acceleration tools at your disposal, it may seem that your business can already run itself. You can already offshore or outsource major and minor tasks, you can automate certain processes and you can have freelancers do other business related activities for you. However, as an entrepreneur, especially in a start-up business, you need to discern when to do it yourself and when to delegate.

The reason why it is still important to personally do the tasks goes beyond cost savings. Aside from the financial rewards, running your businesses at the early stages provides you:

1. Education and experience

2. Responsibility and accountability

3. Direction and immediate resolution

The best teacher in the entrepreneurial world is experience. You can enroll in several business management classes but seeing it up close and experiencing it firsthand can provide you with more education and learning. Whether you are a beginner or experienced entrepreneur, a new business with its new product or service, will have its own unique characteristics and demand. Even if you have similar businesses, chances are, this start up business will have its own personality.

For example, you may hand over creation of the online logo to a freelancer but you cannot just give instructions and think that you are done with your task. If it is your first time, take the opportunity to be involved in the process. Try out the software yourself; make sketches even in a piece of paper or try to revise it on your own when your freelancer has submitted the work. The more you learn about the process, the more independent you can become.

As the owner, you have the command responsibility of the entire business. This means regardless of what happens in the business, whether it was you or a member of your staff who committed a mistake, you are still responsible. Although your employees,

contractor or freelancers are accountable for their own work, you alone are responsible for all their efforts. The same way all profits and successes of your business are credited to you so are the losses and failures. As early as possible, you have to take complete ownership of the business and whether there is praise or blame, you alone have to carry it. You not only have a financial but also a personal investment in the business. While your team may only run the business for the salary, you have a personal stake in the business. In the business, you alone may have the motivation to make the business the best that it can be.

When you are starting a business, not only are the products and the office furnishing and supplies new, the business processes and systems themselves are new and untested. This means that as much as you have planned for the running of the business, there are bound to be errors or mistakes along the way. In a start up business, the longer it takes for a problem to resolve, the greater its impact to the business. You cannot rely on your business manager or staff to make important solutions to major problems. As the business owner, you can make the decision as soon as it is needed.

There is no universal set of rules that you can rely on for running your business, it requires your personal touch and attention. The more you immerse yourself in the day-to-day running of the business, the more you learn and the better you are prepared for its future.

Networking

Networking may be the least of your concern in the start-up business but it is one of the most important tasks that you have to do when you have settled in on your brick and mortar or online store. Your business may be small at first but it can grow provided you are able to get the word out and partner yourself with new contacts.

1. Aside from online networking, you can also do real life networking. It adds a personal touch to your business and gives the feeling of importance to your contacts.

2. Networking is not about attending a dinner party, you are there for business. When you are networking you have to bring with you your business card and a brochure or a tablet that can show off your products or online store. Have a spiel or a short script of how you can introduce your business.

3. Networking is not a sales call but an opportunity to generate interest on your business. As much as possible do not attempt to sell your products, you are there for the connections.

4. Do not attempt to talk to everyone in your list of contacts instead focus on specific people that have the best chances of bringing in business.

5. Show genuine interest not only on the potential for business but also on the person. Keep the conversation friendly and build trust and rapport.

6. Once you have an idea of the profile of your contacts, follow up after 2 or 3 days.

Your Free Gift

Before you start reading conclusion, here's a simple audio version of this book – just as promised!

Please use this web-address.

http://eepurl.com/bufNj1

Conclusion

Product development can be a long and difficult task for any entrepreneur. Fortunately, the technology of today makes the process more manageable for even novice entrepreneurs. Bridging the gap between your idea and its materialization is made even more possible as long as you are guided by the process flow of product development.

Of course, you cannot do everything by yourself and with a limited budget, you may seek cost efficient alternatives to hiring employees that can do the work for you. The various platforms in the Internet can provide you with a huge network of professionals that you may need. Engineers, graphic artists and IT gurus are all available and accessible. On the other side of the product development cycle, manufacturing can also be more cost effective if you can offshore your production needs. Again, you do not have to go to the other side of the globe to look for factories that can serve your need. The Internet will give you access to offshoring options that have been proven track records in creating and delivering your goods to your doorstep.

When you have your business already set up, whether it is a brick or mortar or an online store, you can rely again on technology to advertise and promote your business. At a significantly lower price compared to traditional marketing, you can reach millions of potential customers through the online ads and links. There are several social media that are often free to use that can provide the ad space that you need.

Although, you can automate and delegate most of the business processes, there is still value in getting your hands dirty and doing the work yourself. You can benefit on firsthand experience through education, negotiation and networking.

Entrepreneurship and technology has allowed start up businesses to start and succeed. Take advantage of these whole new ecommerce industry and make your idea come true and claim your profits in your own business.

Huge Thank You and Words of Gratitude!

First and foremost, Thank You for downloading this book. At the end of the day I'm **extremely** grateful for **every** download and **every** purchase. It really makes me smile and motivates me. I wish that every person would put their best forward for the human race. I wish you unlimited mental strength and discipline to achieve your goals and dreams. **Together** we can make the difference.

If you found the information useful I would be extremely grateful if you could write a short Amazon review. It really does make the difference and I personally read every review and take notes. I want to improve my books, so that I can provide more value to other people. I know that my future books will give you the best experience possible.

How to Contact Me

Please contact me if you want to discuss my books or if you have any questions.

transcendencepublish@inbox.lv

Let's make this interesting. First ten people who **contact me** after reviewing this book, will receive a public acknowledgement at the end of my next book. My goal is to create a connection with my readers - it's my own way of expressing gratitude to my awesome readers.